The Poetry of Business

First Edition

Written & created by:
Tracy Lynn Repchuk

Illustrations by:
David G. Repchuk

InnerSurf Publishing

Copyright & Other Stuff

Published by InnerSurf Publishing,
Box 702, Kilbride, Ontario L0P 1G0 Canada
www.InnerSurf.com/publish.htm
Division of Innersurf International Inc.

Printed in Canada.

National Library of Canada Cataloguing in Publication

Repchuk, Tracy Lynn, 1965-
    The poetry of business / written & created by Tracy Lynn Repchuk ; illustrations by David G. Repchuk.

ISBN 0-9731832-0-9

    1. Business--Poetry. I. Title.

PS8585.E756P64 2003   C811'.6
C2003-902930-1
PR9199.4.R46P64 2003

For information about sponsor page exclusive editions or discounts for bulk purchases, contact InnerSurf Publishing at: 1-888-272-8679

Cover created by: **Christopher R. Grove**
of grovegraphicdesign.com

Photograph of author by: David G. Repchuk

Dedication

When you are endeavoring to take a new path in your life, you realize there are many people that helped you get there, whether it was conscious or not. I would like to thank a few, and dedicate this book to them.

Of course, as most do, I will start with my family, Harold and Margaret Broadbent. Born in England, along with my two brothers Roy and Ian, they came to Canada to provide a better life and education for their children. Many sacrifices were made, and hardships endured, but through it all we had a normal and happy childhood.

To the teachers who encouraged my writing from grade one onwards, to college poetry classes that I took as electives, because they weren't necessary for the computer diploma I was earning.

To my friends, who serve as a great support network, sounding board, and who even, when I sound crazy with my ideas, believe what I say.

To the writers and authors of all the books I have read, for which there have been hundreds, who encourage all of us to reach for our dreams, create our own reality, and to trust and have faith in ourselves.

To my amazing husband, soul mate, best friend, Dave, who together we have learned to love, trust, encourage, believe, and most of all dream. We have both found those desires long buried under reality, and dug them up, dusted them off, and let them fly free. We are steadfast in honoring our sacred contract, and are thoroughly enjoying the journey together.

And especially, even though they are too young to be aware, I want to thank my 3 wonderful children, Kennedy, Celestial and Caleb, who inspire me everyday, love beyond comprehension, and whose naïve and innocent outlook keeps me pure in my thoughts and actions. Their fresh new eyes, questioning everything, have taken me back to my beginning, so I could excavate and find my way on the path.

And of course to God, for with him, all things are possible.

Thank you everyone in my life, I am grateful and blessed.
Tracy Lynn Repchuk

Introduction

Welcome and thank-you for sharing my first book with me. I will introduce you to the book concept, and then to Dave and myself.

The Poetry of Business is one, of a series of books for the purpose of introducing poetry and prose in a fun and enjoyable fashion. My hope is to eliminate the barriers and misconceptions carried since high school, and have you take another look at this insightful medium. My goal is to make poetry as mainstream as any other book you would enjoy.

The poetry styles I chose are as varied as the experiences in life, and in business. The poems are short and without excessive verbiage to embellish obvious details. If I can say it in 3 words, I do. I want your mind to excavate for meaning so you resurrect your own personal memories and emotions. Using a marketing analogy, if I only have 8 seconds to get your attention, I had better get to the point.

I chose business as my first release because I have been an entrepreneur since the age of 20. In 1985 I started a software company long before it was a trendy venture, that still thrives to this day. Poetry is everywhere. Whether it's in a business meeting, a new venture, bankruptcy, or your first sale, every moment represents life, and a major portion of the way we spend our day. I have seen a lot, experienced a lot, and ridden the roller coaster of the business industry with both hands in the air.

Whether you're a new venturist or a work-a-holic, I hope you enjoy, and relate to not only the situations I have selected, but to the underlying message that each contains. Stop, look and listen – make sure you're on track, and not just the 'fast' one.

Introduction ctd.

So what does an entrepreneur and a poet have in common. The answer is a lot.

This book is designed to;
- Increase your awareness of poetry
- Increase understanding of a business person and their experiences – so that both poet and business person gain an appreciation of each other
- Demonstrate various poetry styles and formats, including a DOCNOT style I originated
- Help you identify your emotions, fears and misconceptions
- Help you define your goals so that no matter which poem speaks to you within the progressive cycle of your career, you will see by the final chapter where you want to be
- Provide spiritual messages and undertones to improve your opportunistic vibration

Then there was Dave.
When I met Dave I knew he was the one. The soul scream that sends your body into an adrenaline rush. In October of 1992 he moved from Vancouver to Toronto and joined me from a prestigious position and company. Together we grew, honing our skills, with people and together. Married in 1994, we have 3 kids, all born in June, in 1995, 1996 and 1997. Since then our life has evolved, and made us go deep into those childhood desires, the things called hobbies, past times, or others called foolish. And from that we are venturing to become writer, artist, poet, illustrator, cartoonist, with the added dimensions of publisher, web designers, TV personalities, producers, and continued entrepreneurs.

Join us on our journey, with this and other books that will take you through marriage, pregnancy, relationships, travel, children, food, sports and more.

Sponsor Page

For fund raising or customer/client gift, we have a special edition book we generate that contains your advertising on this page. The whole page is yours, right beside the Table of Contents.

Your order gets you discounted book rates, and starts off with an introduction or advertisement direct from your company or organization. Book courtesy of… Thanks for your generosity… We appreciate our clients…

Your logo, message, web page, address, the works – appears right here. Contact InnerSurf Publishing for special pricing and details. It is a great message medium for your business, and lasts a lifetime.
www.innersurf.com/special.htm

An example excerpt would look like this;

Bravo Software Group

Quality custom software solutions since 1985.
www.bravosw.com

Creators of RemoteDesk – eCommerce integrated software from branch offices, sales reps, PocketPC handhelds, even the web for direct order processing into your accounting system.
www.remotedesk.net

"E.Commerce, E.Business, E.DI E.xperts"
Thanks to all of our clients for getting us here!

The Poetry of Business
Table of Contents

Chapter 1: So this is my career

Chapter 2: Wishful Agenda

Chapter 3: Day In Day Out

Chapter 4: The Entrepreneur

Chapter 5: The Perks

Chapter 6: Can I retire yet?

Chapter 7: The way it should be

Illustrations:

Poetry 101 Lessons:

Chapter Contents:

Insights:

Prelude:

Chapter 1

So this is my career

Chapter 1: So this is my career

The Possibilities

Resume Rebound

Apres Education

Is this what I picked?

Compromise is my middle
name

Home away from home

I think the corporate
ladder is broken

Monday's always screw
up my Sunday

I loved my career

The Possibilities

Scanning ubiquitous objectives
endless streams cascade
drenched in opportunity
leaving you refreshed.

Toiling over options
burdened by indecisiveness
exhilarated with variations
you're left dripping.

Surpassed expectations excite
yearning needs beckon
contemplation subdues notoriety
you surrender fearlessly.

Timeless passions smolder
heartfelt indicators accelerate
whispering voices erupt
carelessly demanding action.

Imagination inspires consciousness
reality distills foundation
somewhere between them
serendipity is satisfied.

Resume Rebound

Factual essence permeate crisp white 60 lb. sheets
bold fonts caress with sensual undertones
assets are listed in balance style format
friendly, responsible, eager to please
skills and education conscientiously displayed
while a dash of fiction highlights the expectations

grateful for the biased representation
summarized succinctly with daring flair
irrelevant circumstances defiantly absent
reviewers audit the quiet credit of experience
your lifestyle and personality reflected in its brightest light

you hint for a virtual appointment
petition for a fictitious amount
paint your interview face confidently
hopeful to divert attention from self-imposed obligations

coveted posting is parroted on the linen cover
concluded with conviction you are the finest candidate
you mail it on the way to your sacred spin class

planned, created and launched for success
it's presented in consideration

universally gift wrapped with hope.

Apres Education

Graduation it is over
diploma's on the wall
it's get a job this summer
continue right through fall.

I no longer have to study
my work is what I'll do
from 9 to 5 I will perform
then off out for a brew.

Friday it's a golf game
they network all the time
a meeting to prepare for
in which absence is a crime.

Seminars on the week-end
trade shows till it's late
the extra hours are killing me
I never get to date.

Conferences annually
training until dawn
smile and nod approvingly
and pray that you aren't wrong.

When will this learning ever stop
school is what I yearn
because of this car I just bought
I've got to stay and earn.

Is this what I picked?

Searching for what I'm supposed to be doing with my life
I wonder how I ended in my supposed chosen profession
not a mid-life, birthday approaching, where am I thought
but "Did I ever stop and ask what I wanted" epiphany.

Sitting, staring out the beckoning window
surrounded by a vacant sense of achievement
so far, not thrilled with the outcome
I retrace my evolution for answers.

I smile as high school fondly flashes by
astounded I passed, mystified I survived
my natural obsession of the opposite sex
feeling rushed into decisions too immature to appreciate.

Immune to the auto pilot engaged from college overwhelm
deprived of basic fundamentals, fragments dissolve
ransacked room littered from oblivious evening before
I graduated miraculously with honors.

Fulfillment taunts me from inner depths of recollection
dutiful reminders consume my subconscious
I use to envision being consumed by pleasure and ease
fragile lines of work and play invisibly blurred.

"Hello, yes, okay, I'll be there in a minute."
internal mechanisms activate ambition
implicit doubt triggers complacent momentum
late for a meeting, my optimistic voice quiets

waiting for dynamic thought to actualize.

Compromise is my middle name

When the sales rep needs yellow
and the customer wants emerald blue ones
I give them both green
proudly, I smile.

Optimistic supervisor says bring by 5
obstinate boss demands it promptly for noon
I deliver it at 3
relieved, I smile.

When I request a substantial raise
but the organization's looking to lay off
I accept my new title
graciously, I smile.

Neglected family deserves my loving attention
typical conference on the week-end dictates attendance
understanding family comes for pleasure
joyfully, I smile.

Seeking less commitment to the office
alternately, I am urged to embrace retirement
I accept the voluntary vacation
reluctantly, I smile.

Relaxing on the sultry crystal sands
trendy tourists select one of my loungers
rental fee in my palm
easily, I smile.

Reflectively reviewing the eloquence of affairs
transpired by a life of obedient overtures
compromise is my middle name
satisfied, I smile.

Poetry 101 - Stanzas

Many poem examples in this book use a Stanza format.

A **Stanza** is a group of lines in a rhyming pattern.

There are different types of stanzas depending on the number of lines each has.

Couplet – 2 lines

Tercet – 3 lines

Quatrains – 4 lines

Quintets – 5 lines

Sestets – 6 lines

Septets – 7 lines

Octave - 8 lines

Once you get beyond 8 lines, they are simply called nine-line stanza, ten-line stanza etc.

Home away from home

Disoriented, I raise my flattened forehead from cold steel
remove a reminder and rub my blood shot eyes
hypnotic numbers must have caused me to doze off

distant quiet hum of the air conditioner serenades me
barren office dark, aside from a small strip of fluorescents
rising slowly, my back and neck lock with a knot

grateful, I find a ragged towel hiding in my moldy gym bag
still damp from this morning, compression suffocates
I snap it to life as I walk

tons of uninterrupted hot water seductively cascade
spacious stalls and endless peace captivates my senses
my love affair is strengthened

thick atmosphere is foggy, I'm oblivious of passing time
from a circle etched on the mirror condensation queues
scratching of brittle whiskers echo on concrete

barefoot, dripping, I boldly tread on the dull, matted carpet
hoping fresh socks are among my meager belongings
bruised apple and a crushed energy bar cower underneath

bountiful treasure it is recovered and devoured
I rejoice in my apparent good fortune
on the wall, rigid hands point out my destiny

reminded, I speed dial home as an unfamiliar voice startles
I disconnect determined to avoid the company message
consumed by shame, my lethargic finger manually redials.

I think the corporate ladder is broken

My first job, the fast track, my big break
supporting roles, leading man, stunt double
bright and enthusiastic, a Hollywood star
my Oscar winning performances mount up

one rung higher, the view inspires
expansive, broader perspective realized
appreciating the 'big picture', I dig deeper.

Longer days, critical hours, my credits accumulate
editor, director, producer
compassionate and compelling, reviews enhance status
I expand, rising like a balloon

I eagerly climb, inhaling the altitude
precise, next move executed
with hunger and passion, I search beyond.

Expectations explode, responsibilities rise, my resilience frail
writer, sales, promotions
interesting and witty, concludes the reporter
I empty, as life spills from my pores

pensively I ascend, gasping for air
dizzy, tender stomach tightens
fear of falling down, my knuckles whiten.

Exhausting takes, increased deadlines, my stardom fades
scheduler, gopher, stand-in
bewildered and confused, the mantra beguiles
my footing unsteady, vertigo overwhelms me

slipping I drop, eyes firmly clenched
unrecognizable, true identity vanished
aching to let go, my hands open.

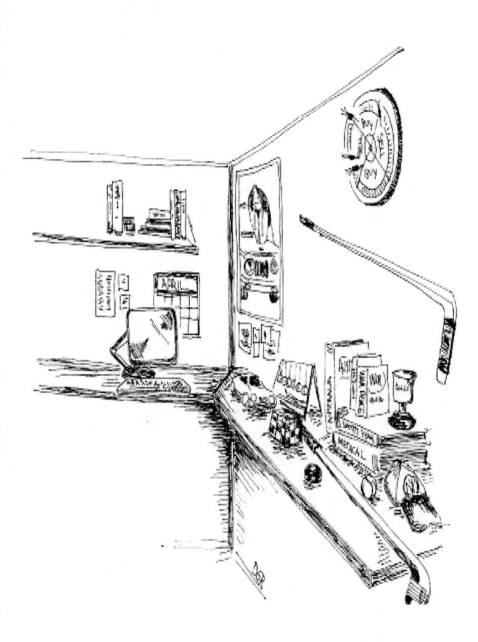

Desert Island

Chapped parched lips
diligently I debate
sacred possessions entice.

Hands tremble nervously
preservation instills knowledge
survival instincts activate.

Self centered transient
hungered by judgment
chosen three rejoice.

Information drowns ambitions
Gideon's medical journal
Friday's illness diagnosed.

Enjoyment informally profound
cork dart board
critical predictions forecasted.

Enlightened energy depleted
deck of cards
promoting life's long-shots.

Proudly I display
humble cubicle complete
inhibited by policy.

Tour of duty
stranded methods employed
S.O.S.

Monday's always screw up my Sunday

Soothing beams of light sear through heavens gate
aching eyes get nourished from its divine opulence
serenity subdues urgency as I melt between satin sheets
just me, the paper, and a steaming cappuccino in bed
a smile caresses me as spirit and conscience collide.

With the fury of shattering glass I'm rudely awakened
that big report is due Monday, and I haven't even started
I leap, heart pounding like an aged marathoner
research, analysis, statistics, diagrams –
all summarized into a riveting PowerPoint presentation.

Mouth dry from last nights indulgence
Listerine swirls with the brute force of a flushed toilet
burnt toast that sat out from the evening before
reheated tar from the bottom of the coffee pot
greeted by the hostile whine of the computer.

Dancing sun blinds the archaic monitor
laughter of children echoes from swaying trees
vibrant cardinals twitter discussing afternoon tea
betrayed shutters close away holistic healing rays
as the glorious day unfolds.

I loved my career

I loved my career, but now that's not true
long hours, dull duties, works' endless queue

It's time I thought harder what to do with my life
I'm unhappy and bored, it's not fair to my wife

Sole purpose or calling, deep questions begin
I search for solutions by looking within

When I was a kid I yearned to do art
my parents said no, so it's the place I will start

True authentic self lives lost inside me
begging and praying to finally be free

I will reduce obligations to discover my soul
make dynamic optimism my thoughtful new goal

Cultivate creativity and open some doors
opportunity's knocking, just answer yours

Remember an era when your world all made sense
when you weren't so distracted, frustrated and tense

Change what you're doing, today's not to soon
your family and friends, will love your sweet tune.

Chapter 1 - Insights

Write down any messages that jumped out at you from Chapter 1, and take a look what these mean to you.

Date: _____ / _____ / _____

Chapter 2

Wishful Agenda

Chapter 2: Wishful Agenda

Rise Shine

Commuters Congo

Caffeine Kickoff

Meeting Meeting

Desktop Depression

Watercooler Boogie

Bored Room

Marketing Mantra

Sales and Sangria

Rise Shine

Buzzing interrupts the fantasy I felt destined to realize
one eye ascends and fixates unsteadily on the sideboard
reluctantly I rise from the enticing covers
flagrantly aware the furnace isn't on yet
hard, stark ceramic floor of the bathroom chills me
I sit, not confident enough for accuracy.

I brush the toxic atmosphere from my morbid mouth
unsteady hand makes me grateful I shaved before bed
groping hopelessly for clothes laid out last night
mismatched socks are an act I don't care to repeat
I kiss my obliviously comfortable wife
who remains rolled in her sausage reprieve.

Through the hall I stumble conscious of the path
but unaware of new obstacles that may lay in front of me
my loyal percolating pot welcomes me
keys jangle, shoes shine, wallet groans upon departure
opportunistically they're thrust into position
faithful chariot ignites heroically to life.

"It's going to be a beautiful day", the radio confirms
on command, protective garage door majestically lifts
streaming beams surround me in cultivating shadows
surreal beacon signifies an optimistic journey
with enlightened radiance from my continued integration
I thoughtfully reverse into the dynamic horizon.

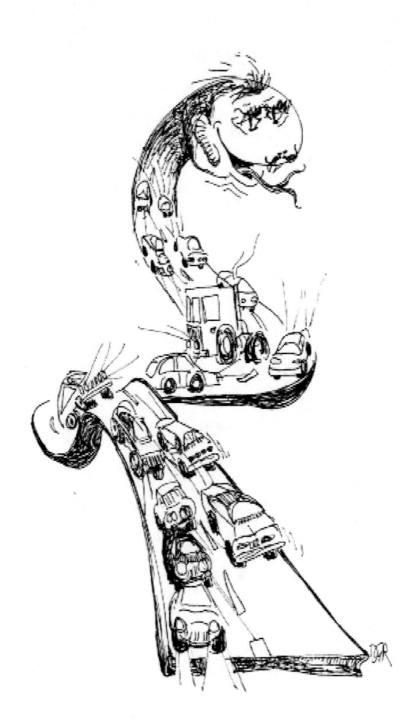

Commuters Congo

Endless miles the white snake winds in sequence
slithering methodically through valleys and hills
sensually the hypnotic dance intoxicates
abruptly stopping with obtuse purpose
bewildered victims arrive then gratefully escape
merging deliberately upsets the delicate balance
alarms echo between hostile transients
fiercely, black venom ignites.

Trance-like eyes seduce you into submission
automatically you continue to rhythmically meander
music temporarily engages the brazen beast
frustrated, distractions provisionally tame
sustenance lay scattered in unstable abundance
still hungry, satisfaction is inadequate
angrily he stands poised to strike
attacking, he warns his unsuspecting prey.

Along shifting horizons the celestial orb beckons
blinded, he shields himself from its powerful sting
unpredictable movements caution the crowd
protruding fangs linger precariously
rattling engines forcefully establish position
searching within, patience sarcastically cowers
destination the sole goal, lost identity sheds its skin
we yearn to surrender, only for the true hunger to begin.

Caffeine Kickoff

3,2,1 and it's ready
favorite mug is passed
skillful snap of the pot
hot dripping liquid is daringly poured.

Black tar-like it moves through sleepy defenses
and is swallowed in a scalding gulp
minor penalty abruptly halts it in mid field
regrettably, it huddles while you dress.

Hiked up, you competently embrace
consumed with the grace of charging bulls
it's slammed on the stained counter
still shaking, determined it gains solid footing.

Substitution is signaled, in comes the new cup
able to travel well
it's filled in mid air
and whisked into offensive traffic.

Through neglect it cools
eager replacement is called from the speaker
the hand off is clean
and the conversion swift.

Poised for action
the roof is raised
thrust from its cozy environment
it's hurled into the sweet zone.

Touchdown catch!
grateful body screams with relief
energetic native dance erupts
and today's game begins.

Poetry 101 - Sestina

Invented in Provence in the thirteenth century, it does not repeat lines, only words.

It is composed of 6 stanzas, of six lines each, and concludes with a final tercet (called an envoy).

The end words get repeated in a certain order, and in the closing tercet, all six words are used.

The format (if designated by the following letters), is as follows;

ABCDEF
FAEBDC
CFDABE
ECBFAD
DEACFB
BDFECA

BE   (closing tercet)
DC
FA

If I were to assign the following words, to the following letters, the following poem **Meeting Meeting** would result.

A = meeting
B = boring
C = endless
D = time
E = late
F = apologize
 (If you want, put a paper along the margin over the letters)

Meeting Meeting

A I constantly feel like we're going to a meeting
B Meeting just to meet is beyond boring
C Speakers drone on, voices and thought endless
D They're incapable of starting on time
E They traditionally go until late
F I wish one day somebody would apologize

F For my unscheduled arrival, I apologize
A Uninvited, I felt this was a critical meeting
E If we didn't address the issue, it would be too late
B I inject energy in a situation that is usually boring
D They ask me back next time
C My regret seems endless

C Bumper to bumper traffic on my way is endless
F I scramble to my seat, wondering if I should apologize
D It figures this would be the occasion it starts on time
A Finance is meticulous about their meeting
B Numbers cascade making it incomprehensibly boring
E Others arrive, unnoticeably late

E The chair of the board anticipates being late
C The agenda is endless
B Doodling in my pad, this is really boring
F The door bursts open and he doesn't apologize
A I got stuck in another meeting
D I'll try not to let it happen next time

D Eager to make up for lost time
E We accept his excuse for being late
A And we proceed with the meeting
C His introduction is endless
F Checking my watch, I apologize
B I have another meeting which will be even more boring

ctd…….

B Are there no meetings that aren't boring?
D Consuming my precious time
F Without the decency to apologize
E Shifting my day to where I have to stay late
C The pile of work on my desk is endless
A Then there's the unscheduled meeting

BE It starts late again, and to no surprise it's boring
DC time seems endless
FA at least for this meeting, somebody finally managed
to apologize

Desktop Depression

Zen in motion you visualize a clutter free zone
breathing deeply in through your nose, out your mouth
eyes open, imagined images violently shatter
stacks, piles, notes, CDs, keyboard, phone
impossibly it thrives on the brink of imminent disaster
amidst the chaos you pluck requested files like a magician
eternally terrified to disturb the mystical balance.

Prioritizing is abandoned in the caverns of remorse
ability to classify or comprehend apocalyptic
mummified, paralysis strikes rendering dementia
you pray for purity from the sewage infested swamps
so you could arabesque across a mine field
escape routes slaughtered as the other world collapses
you debate whether you should bulldoze with brute force.

Infected icons litter the virtual land
screen savers camouflage the insipid hideousness
search and rescue become an art form
defeated, not even Feng Shui could save your soul
only one remedy resonates, continued denial or rebirth
you invisibly desert the suffocating office
and forgivingly commit the whole day to living.

Poetry 101
Personification

Personification is a figure of speech that assigns human qualities and characteristics to something that is not. It is used to provide a different perspective to an event.

An example is **Watercooler Boogie**.

Watercooler Boogie

I stand so majestic
like lady liberty
full of myself
giving liquids for free

in comes Maureen
like a fly on the wall
Guiding Light is her favorite
but she knows them all

Bob he likes football
Joe it's the Mets
Monday's the best night
it's as good as it gets

reality shows
God forbid there's a war
current events
who knows what's in store

a community center
the corporate town square
where meetings take place
and conflicts are rare

everyone comes here
they dance and they jig
holding my hand
it's gone with one swig

the stories they flourish
in the middle is me
a water tank and spout
part of the family.

Bored Room

Long rectangular table hauntingly dominates
agendas and a glass designate each spot
vacant seats diminish
today's show will commence

eager conductor taps his pen
somber hush falls over the anxious crowd
attention spans heighten
velvet plush curtain opens

every performer completes their act
demonstrating artistry in slides and linear charts
historical data renewed
inevitable political debate erupts

crystal water decanters sit empty
flamboyant doodles decorate the otherwise serious pad
margins capture notes
soon to be forgotten

aimlessly my vacant mind spins
decadent high back chair is sinfully comfortable
it induces sleep
wondering eyes slowly close

And that concludes the meeting
Submit your input by the days end
my ears burn
bored room comes alive.

Poetry 101 - Rhyming

Rhyme – the repetition of similar sounds occurring at determined or regular intervals.

Type of rhymes:

Couplet – a pair of rhymed lines, of any length or rhythm ie. Marketing Mantra

End rhyme – near duplication of sounds that takes place at the ends of lines. ie. cat, hat

Imperfect rhyme – a rhyme in which the vowels or sound is similar, but different. ie. own, home; vital, title

Sight (eye) rhyme – words that look as if they rhyme.
ie. through, rough, though

Rhyme Scheme - The particular pattern of rhymed words, indicated by the use of lower case letters. ie. abab

Rhyme Royal - A seven line, iambic stanza with the rhyme scheme of ababbcc

Envelope – this is when 2 rhyming lines are surrounded by 2 other rhyming lines, that enclose it.

A Desktop Depression example would be;

My desk is a mess, a disgrace some would say
I can't find my files, desktop or PC
I'm drowning but there is no rescue for me
I might as well go and have fun for the day

Marketing Mantra

I am the message, straight down from the top
proud corporate culture, the ball you can't drop

repeat me real slowly, say it with heart
believe from the core, that's a good place to start

consistent and clear, now write me in bold
don't ever forget me, you have been told

the web site, brochures, and letter head too
I'm the prominent line, a mission for you

I am the medium, so use me with care
forgetting my place, don't even dare

radio, TV, I want it all
if I'm not the hero, don't even call

I'm in every language, I'm global you know
without my input, the company won't grow

behold me and worship, I'm your chant for the day
for I bring you great tidings, in sales and in pay

so breathe in and out, deeply and calm
I am the master, your fate in my palm.

Mantra Mission

Sales and Sangria

Tall crystal drenched pitcher basks in the sun
cubes swirl in the burgundy passion
sensually invigorating
red cherries joyously bounce

cool satisfaction flows down your malnourished throat
bitter sweetness bathes your eager tongue
enticingly sensitive
your lips seductively savor

erect stir stick conducts an ecstatic symphony
tidal waves crash as it's poured
senses resonate
glasses promiscuously clink together

the carefree frolic of lemon and orange slices
sweet pungency of scarlet consumes reason
scents intoxicate
driven, you inhale deeply

volcanic adrenaline burns as it impatiently surges over
ink to crisp sheets of linen
tingling sensations
bonding, hands ceremoniously shake.

Chapter 2 - Insights

What was your favorite poem in this chapter, and why?

Date: _____ / _____ / _____

Chapter 3

Day In Day Out

Chapter 3: Day In Day Out

I'll check my In-Box
I should be jogging
PDA and other accronyms
Didn't you get the memo?
My briefcase is never
    half empty
Why is it still dark?

I'll check my In-Box

**This poem is a ballad, sung to the tune of Simon & Garfunkels, "I am a Rock".

Sacred pay day
We are waiting for our rewards
Are the pay stubs ready?
And the Granite file is absent
We can't find where it went
He's asking what contractual abstinence meant

I do not know
I'll check my In-Box

Cubicle walls
Small chamber dark and uninviting
That none should impregnate
I have no need for contact
Questions hurt my brain
Always searching for files drives me insane

I do not know
I'll check my In-Box

I have a laptop
And security to protect me
I am hunted by employees
Cowering in my office
Hoping I'm not remiss
They ask me if I've seen Johnson today

I do not know
I'll check my In-Box
Absent knowledge makes me weak
And my In-Box always overflows.

I should be jogging

Co-workers swoon by leaving an exotic wake
like a conga line we add ourselves to the end
herding to lunch

I stop for cappuccino and a biscotti
fumbling for spare change
forgotten gym membership falls out

at home I slump in the chair
index finger professionally poised
settling in on a fitness show

neglected shoes live stuffed in a bag
failing to remind me of my mission
I swear as I trip over them in the hallway

disruptive phone rings just as I reach the door
I settle in to a long awaited call
laces tightened, disappointed soles pout

my briefcase explodes and a file is commandeered
dancing sun beckons as it frolics with nature
rhythmic runner thunders by in sync with my watch

I reminisce as feet and pavement lovingly unite
whining computer prompts patiently for a password
"I should be jogging".

Poetry 101 - Alliteration

An **Alliteration** is the constant repeating of the same letter at the beginning of a series of words.

A famous example of an alliteration is Peter Piper.

Below is an example that I wrote;

Bachelor Brian bought a brown briefcase but broke it buying bonds
The brown briefcase bachelor Brian bought broke buying bonds
If bachelor Brian bought a brown briefcase but broke it buying bonds
Could bachelor Brian bring the brown briefcase broken buying bonds
    back?

PDA and other acronyms

The daunting future of poems
FAQ about your PDA
It's windows
Held in the Palm
96 MB of RAM
Good OCR
Supports HTML
LAN & WAN
FTP to ISP
EMAIL
RFQ on WWW with URL or DNS
KISS
WYSIWYG
TTFN

English Translation:
Frequently asked questions about your personal digital
assistant (Can I get your number?)
It's a PocketPC (costs a lot)
Not a Palm (they're toys)
96 MegaBytes of Random Access Memory (more than your
brain)
Good Optical Character Recognition (I can write it here)
Supports Hyper Text Markup Language (and post it on the
net)
Local area & wide area network (from here and there)
File transfer protocol to Internet service provider (uploads
music)
Electronic mail (to send to my friends)
Request for quote on world wide web with universal
resource locator or domain name server (you can buy a
bride on-line)
Keep is simple stupid (don't be choosy)
What you see is what you get (don't believe the pictures)
Ta ta for now (don't blame me for the results)

Poetry 101 - Refrain

Refrain is a repeated verse within a poem or song pertaining to a central topic. The refrain is usually found at the end of a stanza, but maybe occur between lines.

An example is "Didn't you get the memo?"

Repetend is the irregular repetition of a word or phrase at various places throughout the poem.

An example is "Compromise is my middle name"

Anaphora is the repetition of a word or group of words at the beginning of lines.

Examples are "Where is my Yacht" and "Mid life crisis"

Didn't you get the memo?

Hesitant, I show up late for the meeting
I slither apologetically to the only vacant chair
darting stares pierce through my soul as I arrive
a brave comrade whispers,
"Didn't you get the memo?"

Casually I come in dockers and deck shoes
decadent suits and ties fill the suffocating atmosphere
I sheepishly meander hiding my attire from the office
eyes over the cubicle,
"Didn't you get the memo?"

Methodically I log into the secure computer system
eruption occurs as all my files are missing
worm virus detected we were meant to individually offload
hand on my shoulder,
"Didn't you get the memo?"

Hungrily I head to the somber lunch room
festive balloons and colorful streamers delight
a giant card gets handed to a retiring icon
reading, my friend turns,
"Didn't you get the memo?"

Desperately I rush breathless to my humble desk
table top pristine, boxes stacked neatly in rows
panicked, I scan the environment as my gut wrenches
"Sorry", our eyes lock,
"Didn't you get the memo?"

Poetry 101 - Apostrophe

An **apostrophe** is a poem that addresses something that cannot answer, whether it be an object or an absent person.

If I took my poem **My briefcase is never half empty**, using the apostrophe style, an example would look like this;

I won't lock you my burdened comrade
fearfully embraced by your claustrophobic tomb
with your insides copiously spilling to the floor
do you not wish me to have a life?

Your worn edges make me look old
yet I have only begun to realize my quest
do not assume because we're together I'm your friend
you are simply a reminder of all that must be done.

Regretfully it's time for us to go home
you should sleep until we get there
overwhelmed from the stress of your stagnant contents
I feel obligated to carry you to safety.

I dreamt once that I had left you behind
carefree and unencumbered I skipped to my car
then the image of you penetrated my being
and I could see that you would quiver alone in the dark.

My briefcase is never half empty

Neglected combination displays a null value
locks instinctively click from my permissive touch
bursting seams unhinge weakened clasps
rabid contents tumble to the expansive floor
colored folders remain crushed
a jammed stapler erupts
papers gain consciousness
claustrophobically clinging to life.

Removing the days optimism
breathless goods attempt to flee
fresh air rejuvenates moldy surfaces
embracing new found freedom invokes serenity
daunting pile builds to skyscraper proportions
current residents panic, scanning for available real estate
on bent edges they pray for salvation
knowing their dread will lead to the inevitable.

Pounding alarm repeats from a circular desk ornament
abruptly documents are thrust deep inside
brute force is administered bruising the occupants
swollen, the lid clamps, and is lifted vertically into flight
unprepared arm is shocked into momentary submission
heavy weight champion title restored, it's carried to safety
ceremonious battle won, but not the sympathetic war
wishful celebration for a time when it is only half full.

Why is it still dark?

Methodically entering, I am burdened by the sharp contrast
snow forms a lagoon as I wait for my cubed chariot
vertical thrust from the platform, I retrace inherent steps
archaic Neanderthal I hunch in my lifeless cubicle
preciously shielded from the days unfolding beauty
virtual shackles enslave, safely securing performance
endless hours spent cradled by nurturing florescent tubes
constant companions of the demented internal prison
my eager mind wanders relentlessly scanning objectives
I imagine a fiery sphere spreading rainbow beams
silent ice flakes dance, sparkling until they gather warmth
innocent droplets of dew cleanse and renew my soul
intervening seasons strangle the passionate embrace
deserted environment alerts my subconscious
quiet echoes whisper cryptic messages.

Infused excitement explodes, and I exercise my freedom
with a boot camp mentality I ecstatically flee the scene
abandoning perceived obligations
weightless ankles scurry to unguarded front gates
revolving doors spin effortlessly as I propel myself forward
breathless, panting, city streets pound from the absent din
disappointment swells as I walk religiously to my car
mid-step, eyes toward the starry sky I plead
"Why is it still dark?", with rhetorical abstinence
obvious answers flood my overwhelmed cortex
throbbing spiritual overload, cerebral connection subsides
wearily I drive hypnotically dictated by evolution
unable to see the desired light, I go within to bask in His
vowing to deny history its repeat, I commit to my true path
resolute I travel in my own dimension of dynamic optimism
and dedicate to cultivating new opportunistic thought.

Chapter 3 - Insights

If you could change 3 things about your career, what would they be?

1.

2.

3.

After writing them down, come up with an action for each that would get you one step closer to achieving them.
1.

2.

3.

Date: _____ / _____ / _____

Chapter 4

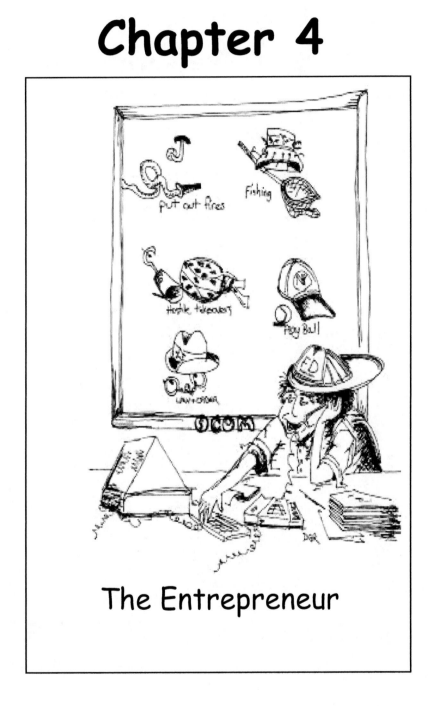

The Entrepreneur

Chapter 4: The Entrepreneur

My own boss
Financial Fuel
Where do we keep the
    staples?
Shoestring Budget
Holidays Galore
But I just went to bed
Just a second, while I
    change my hat
Family Photo
Where is my yacht?

My own boss

I love being my own
boss. I get to say what goes.
I can show up any time I want,
although I arrive in about 6am to get
the day organized. I can go out for lunch
everyday, but I usually brown bag it and
work straight through. I don't have to answer
to anyone, even though the customer is
always right . I can vacation any time I
want, despite that it has been 4 years.
I get all sorts of perks and write-offs,
though the government disallows
most of them. I can
earn as much money
as I need, sometimes
I do skip my
pay to meet
expenses. I
can leave
work early,
but quietly
so my staff
doesn't think I'm a slacker.
I control
my own
destiny,
right after
I make
this
putt.

This poetry style is called **Concrete, where you use the
words to create a picture symbolic of the poem.

Financial Fuel

Business is exploding, more work than staff I've got
I need a fund infusion, gold in a giant pot

self-financing is an option, mortgage my own house
despite the faith she has in me, I wouldn't have a spouse

family, friends, blood money, is good and well for some
this and pleasure just don't mix, says my dad and mom

private investors, angels too, pennies from the sky
the only thing that I dislike, is they take a piece of the pie

banks and trust, lenders abound, paper thick and stale
innovation is new to them, my first born is not for sale

venture capital is on my list, leverage they don't need
but it's a lot they want to know, for money they call seed

Government loans and grants, I laugh aloud in vain
for getting those guys in your life is criminally insane

going public or IPO, now this sounds like a breeze
but everyone is your boss, stock owners you must please

I'm confused, I yearn success, in spite all that I've learned
I hope what I'm about to do won't cause me to get burned.

Where do we keep the staples?

He peaks around the corner
   searching for guidance
     I look up acknowledging
     confused expression
       I point over there.

Face deep in colored files
   fanning their tops
     I approach the cabinet
     blankly staring
       I pluck it out.

Cup in hand he stalks
   caged tiger released
     I open the drawer
     defenses drop
       I produce a filter.

Letter clasped to his chest
   studying cryptic numbers
     I reset the meter
     deep insertion
       I adhere a stamp.

Phone perched on his shoulder
   presses and stops
     I deliver the rolodex
     redialing confidently
       I give him privacy.

Papers separate as he walks
   cursing, he bends
     I grab the stapler
     mutual respect
       I load the staples.

Shoestring Budget

I have just received the greatest idea
by promoting it in advance of its creation
we could materialize it virtually
attracting the required money to manifest it
it's an opportunity not to be missed.

If we use both sides of the paper
lick our own stamps
and borrow pens from hotels
we could envision a one-page flyer.
If we shared a phone
stopped consuming donuts
and fired the secretary
we could embrace a full-color catalog.
If we took a pay cut
moved the office home
and returned the Saab
we could transcend a 30 second TV spot.
If we charge for coffee
rented out desks
and leased back the computers
we could invoke a messenger and
if they believed in the concept
trusted their intuition
and listened to inner guidance
we could all magnetize what we want.

If we take the higher path
follow the design
and duplicate the prototype
we'll all be rich.

Holidays Galore

Traveling to distant lands of exotic destinations
all expenses paid on my own private jet
intrigue and unbridled excitement abound
it's how I dreamed it would be.

My last significant vacation was 4 years ago
a faint memory on an eclipsed horizon
desires trampled, as we couldn't sail to a tropical island
my trusty cell phone wouldn't work.

An adventure trek through the Amazon wasn't possible
my email wasn't available via satellite
no fax support on safari, slow mail in Tibet
incompatible computer connector ruled out Egypt.

So we went to Utah, a lovely hotel with an indoor pool
it rained the whole time, but at least I was away
when we booked Australia, the great barrier reef
a major client had a system failure, and duty called.

Reflectively, there was a large system installation
3 years back it was a milestone project deadline
ironically, I only recall reasons for my clipped wings
voyages spread on blankets like a forgotten picnic lunch.

Now, as I cruise the oceans of the world-wide-web
swing amidst jungles of uncharted territories
I wonder why I envisioned myself to wait for this
grateful, thought turned to the reality of holidays galore.

But I just went to bed

Weak eyes are all bloodshot
my hair a rat's nest
I've been up for days
you can probably guess

stained shirt it is flung
with abandon it stands
sturdy rock of Gibraltar
it thumps as it lands

like paper mache
they practically tear
I rip off worn pants
they don't have a prayer

I brush at my teeth, thick grime does not budge
tar pits in the desert, fearful bottomless sludge

splash on hot water, some places are missed
stood dripping with pleasure, pure wedded bliss

slide into the covers, sink deep with delight
in heavenly sin, on this decadent night

awakened abruptly, alarm that I dread
like a nympho at sunrise, "But I just went to bed".

Benefits are taxable

Medical, personal use of a car, room and board
presumptuously put right back into your income
easy come, easy go

anticipated bonus for surpassing projections
additional hours spent meeting objectives
the more you give, the more you get

unexpected windfall is bestowed upon you
charities queue for your attention
what goes around, comes around

accumulation of great wealth
making sure the less fortunate are remembered
divine laws of reciprocity

free to choose and manage your own destiny
risk of failure, fear of success
dynamics of attraction

visible events are virtual realities
spending means you have it
spiritual payback

inner peace and balance
fulfilling your sacred contract
universal flow.

Just a second, while I change my hat

Good morning,
> how can I help you?

Yes that is possible,
> we can ship directly to you.

It can do all of those things,
> and save you money.

If you uninstall,
> you can re-register on a different PC.

I can open up an A/R account,
> or process on a credit card.

By taking out a lease,
> we can spread your payments equally over one year.

With our commitment to this market,
> we guarantee performance.

Simply attend a webinar,
> our technicians will step you through it.

I can get the staff on that right away,
> these issues will be addressed at the highest level.

Thank-you for your support,
> and remember, I'm listening.

Family Photo

At the left hand corner of my desk sits an elegant picture
guilded case embraces irreplaceable sacred jewels
mountainous stack of folders tower and protect
pink messengers lay skewered like pigs
unopened magazines spill from burdened bins
sticky notes frame the neglected monitor
multiple clocks display times around the world.

Disruptive phone commands and I respond
distant tiny voice from inside wakes my trance
alarmed mind races to identify the sacred source
standing hypnotized, ashamed of thought
putrid lumps grow in my throat
unstoppable tear drops from my naked soul
remorse weakens my buckling knees.

Angered, my arm violently explodes
multi-colored obligations beg for my forgiveness
sprawling helplessly on the aged Berber
I grab the photo and wipe thick dust with my thumb
my stomach heaves as I attempt to balance
valiantly I search for courageous words
as my son asks how my day is going.

My mind urgently scans for critical essence
the core seed of my relentless journey
freedom for every aspect controlling destiny
not to be the marionette I once was, graduated to master
connected soul guides me gently out of my routine
reunited with the power of my integrated memories
I realign with the universal paradigm, and respond.

Where is my yacht?

Keys echo as they land on the vacant counter
turning on forbidden lights my eyes adjust from the shock
cool white chamber beckons with its alluring presence
I search for comfort.

Reheating old pasta, I devour hovered at a gleaming sink
despising its blandness, paprika dances until impact
surrounded by staggering silence
I search for answers.

My plans swirl in dusty bowls as it seductively crystallizes
staring, hypnotic darkness flushes melancholy waste
metamorphic souls interact in slumber
I search for dreams.

To the alert angels I plead, Where is my yacht?
resonating, my own voice captures my thought
repeating questions circle lost parameters
I search for rewards.

Abundance yearning consciously consumes
fingering a cracked tile, loathing its imperfection
pleading for universal acknowledgment
I search for success.

Internal chasms ache for my neglected family
glancing at my watch, Einstein's irrelevance mocks me
through black holes in space
I search for time.

Delicately spooning into my enchanting spouse
I deeply inhale virtual essence of purity
looking inward for divine prosperity
I search for happiness.

Chapter 4 - Insights

If you could work for yourself, what would you do? Don't worry about time, money, obligations, pretend it is handed to you from a complete stranger.

If you work for yourself already, what are 4 things you would like more of. After writing them down, come up with an action for each that would get you one step closer to achieving them.

1.

2.

3.

4.

Date: _____ / _____ / _____

Chapter 5

The Perks

Chapter 5: The Perks

Gross Wages

Sweet Lease

The copier is jammed

Happy Birthday to me

2 weeks with pay

Personal Points

Summer Hours

Stock Options

Now that's a cool title

Bonus Bucks

Gross Wages

Opportunity burrows dynamically precipitating windfalls
wages seep into saturated soil like wildflower seeds
erroneous perception translated by paradigms.

Elusive new promotion parades triumphantly to your desk
monetary incentive seductively hides behind bureaucracy
bittersweet thrills rejuvenate your persona.

Victorious defeat is joyfully trampled by optimism
fallen soldiers heroically strip on the shore
proof thought produces, rewards your essence.

Confirmed business trip accentuates global perspective
extended hours diminish inherent compensation
gratuitously seeing the world.

Loaned credit card that doesn't obligate you
politically governed by philosophical limits
enjoyment without responsibilities.

Co-workers greet you after the week-end
ironically a pay cut kept everyone there
cultivating friendships expand your horizons.

Sacred chance of a lifetime
you would have done it for free
icing on the cake.

Fulfilling desires doing what you want
rewarded by getting paid to do it
payback comes in many flavors.

Sweet Lease

Sweet lease granted prosperously on life
sourced from incarnation or spiritual birth
new term commences, optimistically infused
borrowed time recorded for posterity
gallantly maximizing palpable pleasures
zestfully cruising on the sacred highway.

Basic, subcompact, maxi or upgraded model
features intrinsically added as desired
evolutionary enhanced experience invoked
choices continuously bombard, tirelessly tempt
usage divinely monitored, retroactively empowered
proof of delivery sympathetically recovered.

Confusing directions circumvent hierarchy
guidance system skillfully engaged
unlimited destinations globally personified
contractual obligations predetermined
opportunistic fulfillment optional
substantive penalties dynamically actualized.

Reckless driving cultivates darkened paths
lessons learned hedonistically compose rugged fabric
damages to repair cohesively honor restorations
chosen vehicle inspires distant voyages
reliably fulfilling its ultimate purpose
until expiration suspends the journey.

Critical decisions triggered to disclose enlightenment
thoughts sanction a blessed return or evolved stay
holistic blueprint dutifully reviewed
abandoned objectives plead for renewal
activation of extended warranty obliged
continued exploration universally covered.

The copier is jammed

Corporate culture shocks in a sterilized subterrain
prehistoric politics, fictitious climbing, mindless meetings
intrinsically neglecting the fact you have work to do
systolic benefits shine vehemently in darkened forests
you awake to towering friends who holistically shelter
harsh realities averted as rolling storms strike
computer catastrophe, hardware guys deliver a new one
can't access your files, administrator walks you through
software locks, support team perform artistic magic
your e-mail is absent, favorite chair is broken
no paper in the printer, you need a brochure created
web site needs updating, and the toilet is plugged.

Miraculously saviors swoop in and resolve your issues
then one fateful day, the copier is jammed
lights flash like a Broadway production
humming purr of the giant beast screeches in the jungle
panic stricken tribesman surround the injured carcass
papers copiously crumple to a demanding halt
gentle hands divinely caress the receptive organ
with the finesse of the "The Fonz", it's blessed
reports eject sorted, collated and bound into a perfect gift
satisfaction is bestowed
grateful, you return the favor when your skill is beckoned
reciprocally aware you are someone's angel too.

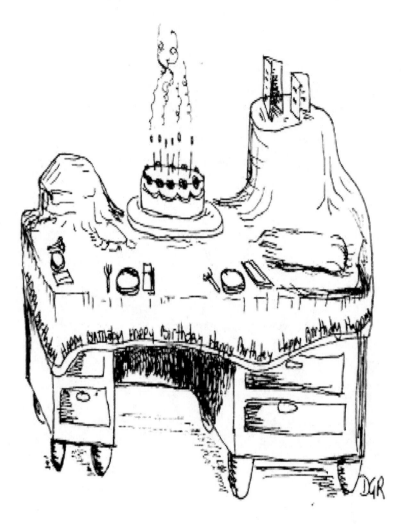

Happy Birthday to me

I tee off as sensual rays warm pristine greens
motorized chariot disguises a pitcher of margaritas
co-workers treat me to martinis and appetizers
abundantly blessed, I embrace their company.

I arrive at my desk to song and cake festivities
blowing out the candles, my wish list evolves
graciously they present a token of camaraderie
soft touching gesture ignites my naked soul.

I end lunch with a specialty coffee and chocolate tort
e-mails build, messages amass, perpetual office turns
throwing the last remnants of the moment in my mouth
I gratefully pause amidst inaudible pleasures.

Reconnecting with my buddy I honor my sacred contract
unite the participating spirits of my dynamic journey
hugging carded words of wisdom from this auspicious day
I depart to celebrate the fact I was born.

Author Moment

At the beginning of the book you may recall in the introduction there could be one poem that speaks to you. The one where you connect, and keep on reading to see where the story takes you.

2 weeks with pay, is that poem for me.

On March 31st I announced to my friends and family that I wanted to write a book by my Birthday, which was April 14th. By time I would pick up the pencil on April 1st, it was 2 weeks away. Impossible they said. I have a software company to run, 3 children aged 7, 6 and 5, plus other board of director obligations.

I chose to spend my 2 week vacation writing a book, plus got paid from my software company. I did it, and I didn't disrupt my lifestyle, write feverishly for hours, skip going out with friends or relaxing on the week-end with my family. It was a pure example of ease, while getting the desired result.

The ultimate message in this poem is that time is irrelevant. It will bend and shift in your favor, so you can get what you want in your schedule. It's as if you put out a frequency, and things fall into place, people come into your life, it simply happens.

I used my mind to precisely guide me when to work to maximize output, with minimum effort.
From the belief of the theory, I now see where I want to be as a poet, entrepreneur and person.
Written as part of an evolutionary journey, I hope once again that you discover your dreams too.

Tracy Lynn Repchuk

2 weeks with pay

2 secular souls intersect to cultivate subliminal thought

wave patterns stimulate triumphant repercussions
enlightenment transcends curious opportunities
enumeration divided equally encourages diversity
kindred reverberations catapult mutual reciprocity
sentient formulas gravitate divine entropy

willingness of faith releases learned barriers
imagination beyond ignites new spiritual connections
thermodynamic analogies crystallize future possibilities
hypothetical leaps defeat mirage-like chasms

payment during growth-overlaps simplify transitions
asynchronous transport through universal portals
youthful invigoration pulsates infinite volts of optimism

2 weeks with pay, what a wonderful way to grow.

Personal points

I fly for the company
and that is just fine
they comp for my travels
but the points are all mine

posh hotel I'm booked at
it's paid, all I do
is present them my card
and get points from them too

my credit debt's huge
but the corporation will pay
I'm getting a juicer
from the points on that day

for all that I'm absent
it's a price she must bear
but I'm out of the dog house
when we're going some where

it's off to Australia
Bangkok and Japan
free with my points
including a tan

all that I spend
on a report to the boss
the money recouped
but the points are his loss.

Poetry 101 - Haiku

Haiku, is a 17 syllable poem broken into 3 lines of 5,7 and 5 syllables respectively.

Originating in Japan, Haiku means "beginning phrase".
The rules for this type of poetry are it must refer to something in nature, and represent a season. It is written in the present tense.

Here are some that I have written;

> trimmed greens invite play
> eagle putt circles and drops –
> I dance with my club.

> soaked under clear skies
> water shoots from the sprinkler -
> dripping in butter.

> virtual market
> glossy brochures fill my cart -
> ripe melons are picked.

Summer Hours

9am, bounding excitedly to my vacuous desk
grateful the sweet taste of summer simmers in the air
patios beckon as we depart for refreshments
reasonably we return for a productive performance
afternoon wanes while dancing mirages urge me outdoors
4pm, we might as well head home.

10am, I examine the brisk agenda in detail
bronzed from my endeavors I bask in memories
eager to share exploits, we congregate for a bite
lost in conversation we rush back to a deserted office
apologetically, we optimize our ethics and morally serve
3pm, leaving early our personal pledge for fun begins.

11am, competitive golf game exceeds expectations
handicapped by a late tee-off the loyal troops rally
meal arrangements appropriately shift in parallel
casually we drop in to pick up neglected obligations
thankfully the boss is absent as our efforts are under par
2pm, we leave anticipating traffic chaos.

12pm, constructive arrival to gather friendly forces
extended lunch permeates the complacent environment
socializing mandate constitutes field work.

Consuming pack for the cottage getaway
journey commences before grid lock possibilities
Friday's a complete write-off.

Poetry 101 – Tanka Senryu, and Renga

Tanka is similar to Haiku, but is the most rigidly adhered to form in terms of structure. It is composed of 5 lines of 31 syllables or less, using a short/long/short/long/long format (5/7/5/7/7).   Overall, Tanka consists of two separate divisions in terms of rhythm structures, each of about one breath length to recite.

opportunities
seized sacred intuition
recognized windows
discovering your purpose
ultimate dream fulfillment

Senryu, or human haiku include only references to some aspect of human nature (physical or psychological) or to human artifacts. They do not address seasons or nature as in primary Haiku.

laughter echoes haunt
axed jobs silence absent friends
listening I mourn

Renga – is a continuation on the Haiku philosophy. It is a Japanese linked poetry style, consisting of 100 stanzas, composed by multiple poets at a single sitting. Each stanza of the Renga is like a link in a chain.

It often starts with a Haiku format of 5,7,5 (3 lines, # of syllables) and the next poet will add a 7,7 (2 lines, 7 syllables each) stanza. The cycle is then repeated.

Stock options

Options, everyday path decisions
opportunity recognition moments precipitated by action
rendering maximum output for efficient effort

remunerated with stock over pay
trust in your divine intuition
risk of becoming an instant millionaire

opening channels to others
kindred beings cultivate heightened experiences
producing deepened synchronous existentialism

progressing your relationship to the next level
holy union publicly acknowledged
sanctioned life time of venerable growth

having children, giving birth
discovering unconditional optimism and spreading it
lasting legacy to the world

looking inward to sanctify your journey
actualizing serenity to share dynamically among others
freedom to be you

identifying your sacred purpose
ignited soul propels towards spiritual enlightenment
universal connection globally expands thought

Einstein's Theory of Relativity simulated
erotic black holes supplemented by new white souls
payoff singularity beyond the scope of imagination.

Now that's a cool title

When money's at a premium
a waste to ask for more
you search for a solution
something never done before

How about a bigger space?
an office of your own
but that is of no use to me
I work out of my home

parking spot right by the door
mere inches and you're there
leave it for the elderly
out of respect and being fair

brand new car on lease for you
a Lincoln or a Vette
I take the bus, is your reply
it's safe and a good bet

membership to a gym
get your body tight and buff
I'm happy living like I do
exercise appears too tough

I think I know just what you need
"Creativity King" is vital
you beam and jump up from your chair
Now that's a cool title!

Poetry 101 -Abcedarian

Abcedarian is a poem having versus/words beginning with successive letters of the alphabet.

An example would be;

ABCs of an entrepreneur

Agile boss creates dynamic environment
factory grows highlighting justification
keeping logistics maintained nightly
operations produce quality refined systems
tracking universally variant wares
Xeroxing you zillions.

Author Moment

You know what I like about the word entrepreneur, it intrinsically does not represent a gender.

Bonus Bucks

Hungrily you input the numbers
adding, subtracting, and multiplying complex columns
invigorated mathematician developing a theory

late night drinks
early morning meetings
smiling at objections

researching the competition
empathizing their plight
providing the edge

demonstration of features
achieved bottom line
synergistic adrenaline rush

anticipation of success
shaking hands connect
beneficial deal sealed

successful delivery coordinated
satisfied customers catalogued
repeat the above

basking in the enlightened quarterly report
rewards of a proven formula
Pythagorous would be proud.

Chapter 5 - Insights

What are the top 10 things you love about what you do?

1.

2.

3.

4.

5.

6.

7.

8.

9.

10.

Date: _____ / _____ / _____

Chapter 6

Can I retire yet?

Chapter 6: Can I retire yet?

Mid-life crisis

Downsizing Dilemma

In the beat of the jungle,
   I feel like an ape

I'm too old for this

Eloping is trendy

Notworking Opportunities

Political Polka

All my friends are
   millionaires

RRSPs are improperly named

My kids can pay for their
   own education, I did

Mid-life crisis

I am an opportunity
Evaluation period for everything you are doing
Get empowered.

I am a celebration
Invite change for the better
Achieve growth.

I am a choice
Release scarcity, embrace abundance
Enjoy today.

I am a gift
Appreciate your unique genius
Become grateful.

I am immensely powerful
Recognize that fear is self-imposed
Without limits.

I am a responsibility
Consequences that truly matter
Discover you.

I am a metamorphosis
Find your voice and ignite the universal life force
Amaze yourself.

I am a crisis
Welcome me, go now
Be transformed.

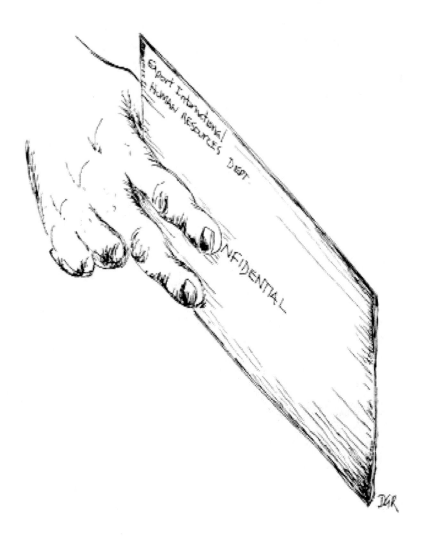

Downsizing Dilemma

Colored graph in the silent boardroom reflects the mood
suffocating atmosphere fills thick with dread
conditions without hope

searching, scanning, historical predominance remains
embarking to appear occupied, futile resistance
questions without answers

globalization, terrorism, war, policies preoccupy
wondering if resolved differences would resuscitate
excuses without reasons

inevitability looms large within diatribe confines
peer evaluation, elevating personal accolades
judgment without purpose

somber shepherd gathers his expectant flock
soulful eyes reveal burdened obligations
duties without joy

environmental reflections defy fearful tyranny
positive infusion catapults arrant beliefs
success without worry

optimistic journey launches on a thoughtful path
dynamic opportunities cultivate new growth
faith without proof

In the beat of the jungle, I feel like an ape

My swollen knuckles drag on torn pavement
passing the staunch security guard, soundless utters grunt
crowded lobbies spill into tiny boxes
bees exit, picking up pollen slows our flight
within rows of tight honey combs I choose my tree
Crouching hidden, I mark my territory.

Commanding pulse echoes from invasive vents
emitting a subliminal drone it distorts thought
ripe banana rings and I devour it with passion
pounding my chest, I dutifully deliver the notes
undulating, a pride of lions parade by to respond
dominant male roars, and we passively cower.

Hurried chatter of chimps increase the rhythm and tempo
busy jungle, mandatory performance guarantees survival
I climb down from my branch, alone among peers
parrots, tigers, bears, instinctively cultivating diversity
beyond function, I plead for democratic socialization
equality aspiring individuals gravitate as one.

Amidst the symphonic beat the kingdom implodes
miraculously oscillating, harmoniously tranquil tribe unites
evolution advances existentialism
dynamic connections cultivated, opportunities astound
optimism emerges in a civilization universally eclipsed
and from singularity, polarized prophets circumvent time.

Poetry 101 - Villanelle

A **Villanelle** consists of 2 rhymes (A,B) and 2 repeating lines that also rhyme. It's scheme consists of either 5 tercets and one ending quatrain, or 5 three-line stanzas and one four-line stanza with 2 repeating lines (C,D). It's roots go back to Italy, but was popularized in France.

Below is a Villanelle I wrote for the poem to the right. To help understand the layout, I have labeled the 4 varying types of lines as A,B,C,D.

C   My hands are too weak to climb this today
B   the corporate ladder has taken its toll
D   I'm losing my footing, don't fall I pray

A   while they climb over I have no say
B   to the top is their ultimate goal
C   my hands are too weak to climb this today

A   political games and hired guns are the way
B   circumstances diminish my role
D   I'm losing my footing, don't fall I pray

A   years have passed by and I don't want to play
B   my life and career through a hole
C   my hands are too weak to climb this today

A   fear has forsaken, a price I did pay
B   swirling and flushed in a toilet bowl
D   I'm losing my footing, don't fall I pray

A   I'm ending this act, it's too wrong to stay
B   inside I search to retrieve my soul
C   My hands are too weak to climb this today
D   I'm losing my footing, don't fall I pray

I'm too old for this

Wrinkled hands   are often shaky
dim eyes too   weak from use
seeking help   from healing Reiki
     my soul ignores a truce
good sleep   is getting random
rising constantly   to pee
light and dark   in tandem
I don't   recognize me
  stained false teeth sit in a mug, each morning in they go
fake hair I brush   is called a rug
tired body   moving slow
Thin air up here   deflates my lung
  I'm only in their way, clinging to this splintered rung
they climb over   every day
perhaps it's time   I cleared a spot
  and left this company, a fallen apple left to rot
no longer   in harmony
I should be somewhere   nice and warm
     troll fishing from my boat
not weathering out   this tragic storm
where they have me   by the throat
  I've decided to end this act, the show it must move on
against myself the   odds are stacked
to stay would   just be wrong.

Eloping is trendy

We spent your planned dowry
on the pool house last year
with no beau in sight
we thought we were clear

Your announcement is thrilling
but more of a shock
your coveted hope chest
we put it in hock

Fragile stock market crashed
hopeful dividends dried
one shot in Las Vegas
we let it all ride

Minister and witness
we've made it easy
a chapel and ladder
holy matrimony

Weddings are stuffy
with months to endure
by time it approaches
you're not even sure

A gown and a tux
some flowers to arrange
a big smile for the photo
and "I do's" you'll exchange

So you see darling daughter
you'll thank us one day
eloping is trendy
just throw the bouquet.

Notworking opportunities

Escorted events, slyly I smile, seemingly socializing
for the sake of the company I endure my obligations
dreary dinners, mundane meetings, veteran volunteering
to get new contacts, secure sales, or personal promotion.
Now I simultaneously strive for enlightened opportunities
preferably not working.

Teeing off on my own terms, phantom play with philosophy
heavenly homebound afterwards to a family that rewards
decadent dining with favorite friends, receptively relaxed
full of complex conversation that emphatically energizes
week-ends away, refreshingly romantic, invigorating
without professional performance.

Agile agendas determine destination desires
glass of Chablis, we arouse amidst brazen brochures
tangent time donated to causes that serendipitously speak
where I hedonistically help, and I'm nobly needed
skillfully serving generosity, thoughtfully granting guidance
kindness and abundance autonomously available for all.

Wistfully I wonder if overt optimism would have mattered
perhaps notorious networking would instinctually integrate
prophetic people transferring mental messages
altruistic actions miraculously maximize worldly wisdom
soulfully savoring a dynamic lifestyle, cultivating creativity.

Focusing on my spirit, I embrace my sacred self
grateful for the paradigm that made me look
I've discovered it was always mine to have.

Political Polka

Motivated, I reveal my solution to the supervisor
fundamental restructuring will precipitate improvements
Brilliant, he says, I'll take this to the next level
the
manager extols its hierarchical infrastructure
minor modifications alleviate dependent strategies
diligent director will be relieved, the problem was unique
original
systematic approach, he admires, embracing its depth
remove perceived bias, categorize distilled steps
accounting will evaluate for indigenous
concept
aroused accountant fulfills a feasible prophecy
cost reductions circumvent budgetary pressures
savvy vice-president heard the rumors already
has
progressively embellished virtues, unjust representation
characteristic feature additions accentuate marketability
universal understanding of investment potential this has
been
completely unobstructed by prominent deficiencies
if you're sure we need it, president approves dynamics
duplicates are sent back to engineering to proceed
entirely
without delay, sanctimoniously it survives sadistic scrutiny
between interpretations and incomprehension's
the original concept has been entirely
lost
ceremoniously the task is absurdly assigned to me
you had better get started he says, It was your idea.

All my friends are millionaires

All my friends are millionaires
How did it get this way?
I work hard to pay my dues
When will it be my day?

I was dot com before the trend
I had to watch the farse
ideas beyond rhyme or thought
money up their arse

They came in droves just to invest
grants and angels too
my product's ranked among the top
no, we want something new

Fancy houses, pools and trips
and now a green Jaguar
shacks, a hose, or to the store
in an old hand-me down car

Companies have since gone bust
short term success and fame
the toys and trappings still in tact
life's a joyous game

Simple pleasures I hold dear
my family's number one
be mindful of your purpose
and everything else will come.

Poetry 101 - Rondel

Rondel – consists of 13 lines, of 4, 4, and 5 respectively. It forms around 2 rhymes, and the refrain is set up in the 1st two lines of the stanza. If possible, it is up to 8 syllables per line.
Format is: ABab abAB abbaA - with respect to rhyme and refrain (repeating line).

An example of **RRSPs are improperly named** would be;

RRSPs are a mean kind of joke
only tax cut incentives remain
at the rate this increases I soon will be broke
my savings gone straight down the drain

Cinders in ash I give it a poke
but my efforts are all done in vain
RRSPs are a mean kind of joke
only tax cut incentives remain

Up through the chimney, a black cloud of smoke
my stomach doubles over in pain
grey matter spills out of my brain
now I'm worth more if I croak
RRSPs are a mean kind of joke.

RRSPs are improperly named

Funds preserved in a Registered Retirement Savings Plan
RRSPs, reflectively roll off your tongue into vacant air
memories of a tax break, decreased to a fractionate value
crippled benefactors helplessly beg for superfluous scraps
prospective retirees labor excessively to recoup losses
sybarite dreams vanish under fathoms of asinine concepts
misguided aspirations collapse false foundations
logical policies propose a necessary name reconciliation
radical selections resurrect dynamic indulgence
relying on acrostic dimensions, evaluation proceeds
Reactivate Really Sucky Pension
Rational Reduction Skillfully Poached
Rare Reality Shows Profit
Ransacked Recovery Salvage Price
Randomly Rape Savvy People
Rather Reinforce Saddams' Pockets
analysis precludes my money be diverted to a mattress
safely secured using intuition and relevance
lessons in living for the moment exemplified
reflecting, I design a tariff free society of optimistic order
consume and earn in equal ratio as supply and demand
opportunistic thought cultivates a retirement lifestyle
when mystic realists deploy permanent prophetic wisdom
ordaining prolific restitution of organic synthesis of life
crystallizing a new optimism to Relax Renew Spend Play
that's the only plan I'm signing up for.

My kids can pay for their own education, I did

Longingly I embrace tempting tickets
hard working, loyal, deserving of financial reward
determined not to crack from self-imposed pressures
bureaucrats whole-heartedly swallow the lions share
bills consume the remaining minority
pleasures spill into dainty reservoirs

Institutionalized wisdom precipitates monetary kidnapping
Registered Education Savings Plans promote urgency
pedantic children uniquely born into makeshift retirement
lethargic youth dismiss gainful repudiation
hefty allowances for just being themselves
inflating the demand for CDs and movie passes.

Eliminating the responsibility of planning their own future
yet granting all the privileges that go with it
precluding the concept of days wrapped in mediocrity
planet high school rotates around a dualistic mentality
single-minded saviors devour weak animists
initiative collapses under a social calendar.

Summer traditions; painting, mowing lawns, pumping gas
training grounds for real world sacrifices, made redundant
RESPs silently obligate guardians into paving their path
proudly I proclaim on behalf of all guilt-ridden parents
"My kids can pay for their own education, I did"
while we shamelessly board our flight to France.

Chapter 6 – Insights

If you were retired, or are retired, what would be/is the top 5 ways to spend your time?

1.

2.

3.

4.

5.

Describe what your retirement party would like.

Are you doing anything to make that a possibility?

Date: _____ / _____/ _____

Chapter 7

The way it should be

Chapter 7: The way it should be

Virtual Office
Special Delivery
Satisfaction of the soul
Welcome to the family
    business
What day is it?
Leave me a message
Golden Handshake
Wishful Agenda
And the award goes to...
Yacht encounters of the
    third kind

Virtual Office

I have no walls that surround,
no ceiling to limit my flight.
Without restrictions,
located where I am

I do not have a cubicle,
no desk where I am chained.
Elements of clutter do not define me,
thoughts flow transparently.

Opportunistic windows are not a mirage,
distant reminders of freedom,
where birds glide and soar,
eternity is my view.

New computer does not greet me
with optimistic gestures of a relationship.
Friends and strangers cultivate,
I am blessed.

Phones do not wake me,
arms folded across my chest
infinite possibilities multiply,
peacefully I meditate.

Manuals do not sit on my shelves,
shallow answers with little dynamic.
Old acquaintances beckon,
graceful words incite passion.

While setting up my office today,
it occurred to me.

Poetry 101 - Cinquain

Cinquain, is a 5 line poem, with 2, 4, 6, 8 and 2 syllables in each line respectively. It was developed by Adelaide Crapsey.

Below are examples to existing poems written in a cinquain fashion.

Virtual Office

Freedom
it has no walls
located where I am
I bring only thought and passion
today

Special Delivery

Open
dreams magnify
sacred contract embraced
awakening actualized
thankful

Special Delivery

Realizations magnify plain truth
simple steps clarify the creation of reality
open, to opportunity

arrival of a package
everything flowing in perpetuity
direct, from heaven

insightful discovery of your unique genius
development of dynamic dreams
delivered, against odds

you give, having more
enjoy freedom, spending time wisely
thankful, of blessings

energetic vibrations form new phylogeny
intuitive thought cultivates continuous optimism
sent, special delivery

breakthrough of realms
enlightened awakening invigorates
actualized, on earth

programmed to receive
acceptance of your true self
sacred, contract acknowledged

desires engulf
plucked like apples in Eden
infinite, abundance embraced.

Satisfaction of the Soul

Waves sparkle majestically as they swoon
mesmerized by soft translucent water
decadently licking the soles of my feet
eyes closed, I worship thought

opportunistic baby emerges from the canal
pure, innocent, soul still connected
it injects inner peace to the witnesses
hands clasped, I embrace myself

coffee beans permeate as they're ground
dancing inside the glass cylinder
they invite me to jig with them
nose alerted, I inhale passion

pristine delights boast on a platter
merged in perfect harmonic balance
tastes cultivate sensually as genetic programming initiates
mouth anticipating, I gulp hungrily

dynamic birds echo in lush forests
enlightened by new melodic tunes
encrypted messages unfold from quiet, optimistic voices
ears resonating, I listen beyond

spirits fearlessly soar unburdened by form
aligned essence just to be
striving to do what I instinctually desire
head upwards, I am free.

Welcome to the family business

My daughter asks what will I do today
I'll see how I feel is what I say
her flowered dress swirls as she goes off to play

What ya' doing?, my boy bellows from the hall
I'm writing, I respond, as I return his call
he curls in beside and drives his car up the wall

My eldest quietly enters, Are you working right now?
surrounded by poetry, I nod, aware of vow
she picks up a book and recites what I allow

Can you get us from school?, they inquire as they rush
I'll collect you at 4, hurry or you'll miss your bus
radiance of their smiles makes me humorously blush

Did you build that? my son stares, blowing his mind
web pages upload, all the same kind
his body drapes over lovingly from behind

My 3 children congregate and draw at my feet
What is your job?, my middle child has to repeat
it took many years, but here is my treat

Welcome to the family business, my sweet young ones
where you do what you love and the abundance tap runs
create and be open, and fulfillment just comes.

What day is it?

Years of dreaming realized
Einstein's theory methodically applied
living in accordance to universal laws
answers lie within, cultivated by thought
my mind wakes and I frolic with the heavens
I use celestial orbs as they rise and set

Following guidance amidst the eternal abyss of conflict
stars chatter, while Galileo and Copernicus lend a hand
a quiet fatigue envelops my receptive body
I meditate as I nap, oblivious to protocol
floating by my translucent cord, new opportunities thrive
dynamic rest renews my optimism as the cycle revolves.

My vacant stomach growls for deserved attention
succumbing to my mood I hunt palatable pleasures
barren cupboards remind me of absent obligations
crammed aisles in stores make me wish I went yesterday
in rhythm with natures call, I relax on a porcelain throne
contemplating, refueling from wisdom between pages.

Strolling with my visions my exquisite journey unfolds
buskers perform, actualizing their outdoor fantasy
polite stranger turns to me in a crowded town square
"Excuse me, do you have the time?"
I nod apologetically, then tap him back
seeking today's message I ask, *"What day is it?"*

Leave me a message

I need the quarterly report
putting on the 9th hole

Get together for drinks?
sailing at the Granite Ridge Yacht Club

Why isn't your cell on?
lunch at café Leone

Can we get an estimate on that?
raking the leaves

What time are you expected back?
sharing ice cream at Yarmouth beach

Call me when you get in
favorite movie at an afternoon matinee

A reminder your car needs servicing
on the treadmill at the gym

Leave me a message
I'm unavailable to take your call at the moment.

Poetry 101 - Acrostic

Acrostic poetry is a form of short verse constructed so that the initial letters of each line taken consecutively form words on the left hand side of the page. The term is derived from the Greek words *akros,* "at the end," and stichos, "line."

If I take the Golden Handshake poem as an example, it would look like this;

Golden Handshake

Grand gestures scintillate
Opportunities between two
Lucid optimism achieved
Dynamic destiny acknowledged
Evolutionary journey cultivated
No contracts required

Honor of thought
Awareness arouses intuition
New venture confirmed
Decisions on faith
Spiritual connection successful
Heavenly oneness verified
Acceleration upward granted
Kindred spirits unite
Enlightenment propels humanity

Golden Handshake

Early times
handshake represents confirmation
acceptance of a term

promises made
no contracts required
unconditional respect between two

opportunities arise
acknowledgement of responsibilities
faith in ones decisions

next level
recognition of efforts
belief in your destiny

request granted
successful ventures accumulate
evolutionary journey accelerates upward

intuition ignites
awareness and growth
burden of proof removed

spiritual connection
universal oneness verified
questions asked and answered.

Poetry 101 - DOCNOT

*This next poem is called a DOCNOT. It is a style we created and labeled that contains 9 levels.

DOCNOT stands for **Dynamic Optimism Cultivating New Opportunistic Thought**, and is our life philosophy for the cycle of actualization. More: **www.docnot.com**

This poem was constructed in the DOCNOT fashion from Chapter 2, hence the name Wishful Agenda.

Left-hand columns source emotions from the inner child.

Level i - The left-hand column describes the sequence of responses and emotions that you experience with respect to the dynamic (Level ii) and actual event (Level iv). Write how it makes you feel. **Ecstatic and pleased**

Level ii - The right hand column is a sequence of steps or elements of the poems actual event, but when combined with the originating poem or series concept, and Level IIII inner child request, you reveal the **dynamic event**.

Desire: Sign right here – "I am the message straight down from the top" Poem source: Marketing Mantra

Level iii - Read each sentence together. The left-hand describes how the right-hand event can make you feel.

Example: sales chant makes you feel driven

Level iv - Read the last sentence. The left sentence is the physical inner child desire request to complete the actual and dynamic event. By combining the cultivating energy with the dynamic event you reveal the essence for the new opportunity. **Sign right here – to close a sale using positive desire for optimism**

Level v – The right hand word from the poems' title is a physical event or manifestation that is used to achieve the opportunity. Get dictionary definition.

Agenda – list of things to be dealt with

Wishful Agenda

Passionate, proud culture
Eager, bold message
Seductive, fate master
Sensual, prominent line
Ecstatic, palm language
Promiscuous, global input
Driven, sales chant
Tingling, calm hero.

Sign right here, mantra mission.

Levels continued below ....
Level vi – The left-hand word from the poems' title is the emotion you invoke or could invoke to respond to Level V with the feeling applied from Level I. Reveals the **cultivating energy**. Select definition from dictionary.
Wishful – positive desire, optimistic
Level vii - The right hand side of the sentence is the name of the corresponding picture. When combined with Level IIII it produces the physical requirement for success, and with the definitions of the words formulates the **new opportunity.   Mantra mission = Mission goal is achieved by getting them to sign right here.**
Mantra – the use of concentrated sacred words
Mission – specific task or duty
Level viii - Looking just at the picture from the surface, what is the actual event?   **Closing a sale**
Level ix - Put the whole poem and picture into one dynamic optimistic thought that uses the cultivating energy with Level V and the opportunity. **If you have a desire and passion to get it done, you can achieve anything.**
(viii)Actual Event: Closing a sale   **(ii)Dynamic Event:** messages from above **(vi)Cultivating Energy:** positive desire for optimism **(vii)New Opportunity:** spiritual messenger sent to deliver a message

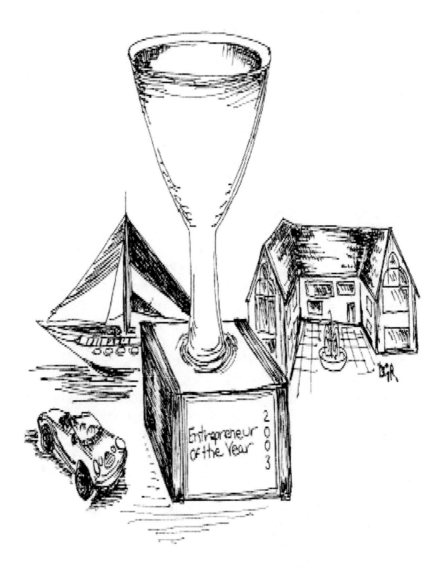

And the award goes to…

Every year you are in business
and doing what you love
it's just the kind of payback
you've been dreaming of

profits soar and wages rise
holidays galore
happy staff, you are revered
makes you grateful to your core

glamour, glitz you have it all
a Mercedes in the lot
big house, pool and a boat
wars were won and fought

kids are at the finest schools
it's the recognition that you need
press releases, interviews
you have done well to succeed

fun and friends is all you want
a loving family too
you count your blessings every day
for such a loyal crew

then one day in comes the call
you've won to your amaze
you thank God and lucky stars
for this great award day craze.

Poetry 101 - Limerick

A **limerick** is a 5 line poem, composed of an iamb and an anapest, and is often of a whimsical nature. Lines 1, 2 and 5 rhyme with each other, and lines 3 and 4 rhyme with each other. Lines 1, 2 and 5 all have 3 feet, and lines 3 and 4 both have 2 feet. The only exception is you can substitute an iamb for the first foot in any line.

Iamb – is a 2 syllable sequence in which the stress or accent is on the second syllable. It is a rising foot.
ie. today

Anapest – is a 3 syllable sequence, in which the first 2 syllables are unstressed, and the third syllable is stressed. It is a rising foot. ie. formally

Feet – poetry was made up of a meter, and a meter is made up of poetic units called feet. The most common types of feet are, iamb, anapest, trochee, and dactyl.

Trochee – opposite of iamb, it is a 2 syllable sequence, stress is on the first syllable, and it is a falling foot.
ie. heaven

Dactyl – opposite of anapest, it is a 3 syllable sequence, in which the first syllable is stressed, and the last 2 are unstressed. It is a falling foot. ie. tenderly

Yacht encounters of the third kind – is a limerick example I wrote.

I think it is a nice way to end your journey through this book.

Yacht encounters of the third kind

A big yacht it is put up for sale
for the owner was sent back to jail
he took money from staff
now he's feeling their wrath
as they bought it for one-tenth retail.

They went out for a sail that same day
having fun with the waves they all sway
while on deck they did see
green men chugging black tea
and they waved for them to come and play.

A round saucer with lawn chairs on top
word was sent for a hatch door to drop
when invited aboard
drinks were instantly poured
as they toasted their union with pop.

The sleek ship was majestically made
and they joked about making a trade
so the creatures said swell
and agreed what the hell
then went off to the yacht while they stayed.

Chapter 7 – Launch Party
Congratulations, now enjoy your journey.

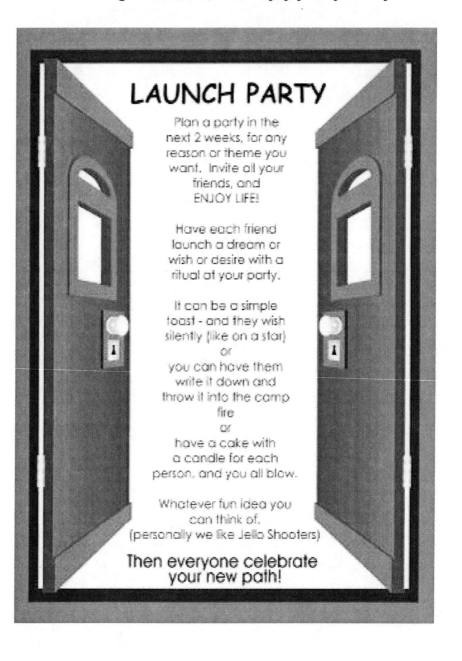

LAUNCH PARTY

Plan a party in the
next 2 weeks, for any
reason or theme you
want. Invite all your
friends, and
ENJOY LIFE!

Have each friend
launch a dream or
wish or desire with a
ritual at your party.

It can be a simple
toast - and they wish
silently (like on a star)
or
you can have them
write it down and
throw it into the camp
fire
or
have a cake with
a candle for each
person, and you all blow.

Whatever fun idea you
can think of,
(personally we like Jello Shooters)

Then everyone celebrate
your new path!

Sneak Peak - The Poetry of Travel

Coming soon is **The Poetry of Travel**. In the same spirit as this book, it will examine the various elements of travel such as destinations, packing, backpacking, kids, food, cultures, accommodations, planes, trains, automobiles, buses, boats and camels. This book will journey you throughout the continents, and with humor in tow, will allow you to appreciate why we always want to get away, and why we can't wait to get home.

Below are chapter examples of what you can expect in this exciting tale of travelers.

Chapter 1 – I can't wait to get away

Chapter 2 – Panicked Preparations

Chapter 3 – Are we there yet?

Chapter 4 – Beds & Breakfasts

Chapter 5 – Holiday Happenings

Chapter 6 – 2 weeks later

Chapter 7 – Life is a vacation

When you register (see last page), you will automatically be informed of new books, events and author updates, including the release date, and pre-release opportunities for The Poetry of Travel.   Enjoy the journey!

Coming soon: www.innersurf.com/poettravel.htm

Poetic words sung

I'm thrilled when somebody has the ability to write great words, but when they have the talent to back it up with music, composition and voice, it is simply astounding. Pat Hewitt is such a person. Pat is a singer, songwriter since 1972 and his passion, style and enthusiasm make every facet of his expressive words even more tangible.
Below is a preview of his new song/poem that will appear on his next CD, 1000 Lost Weekends. Copyright 2003 Pat Hewitt

GAINFUL UNEMPLOYMENT
Sun over my shoulder, coffee in hand-
No map in my car, and no clue where I am
Totally lost and it feels great-
In life without commitments it's kinda tough to show up late!
Cell phone's in the garbage, e-mail got the yank-
Left my pager swimming at the bottom of a fish tank
Demons stashed back under my bed-
Man it felt good just to pull the plug and empty out my head!

I am now a man with a mission in life-
To do just exactly what the hell I like!
A man with passion in life-a man with a plan
To love this life living exiled from working man's land!!

Took a pass on traffic, took a pass on stress-
Took a pass on toiling over someone else's mess
Sleeping in the back seat away past noon-
And if this ain't heaven, man, I'll probably drive thru it soon!
Said goodbye to bottled cures for the stresses of life-
Goodbye to mortgage payments and all my ex-wives
Said goodbye to the boss and the damn minute hand-
Gainful unemployment is the only job I want to land!

To find out about appearances or to hear this song visit:
www.pathewitt.com

Author & Illustrator Biography

Tracy Lynn Repchuk

Born in 1965, nee Broadbent, Tracy has had an entrepreneurial and literary spirit since an early age. Writing poetry since she was 12, it was an expressive constant in her life.

Educated at Sheridan College she graduated with a computer diploma and combined that with her Certified Management Accountants (CMA) designation to launch her first company Bravo Software Group, at the age of 20.

Searching for meaning almost 17 years later her poetic flair was ignited and she opened DOCNOT Gallery as a distribution network for the combination of her poetry and David's paintings, and InnerSurf International, which is a spiritual portal.

With a 2 week self-imposed deadline she produced her debut book "The Poetry of Business", then awaited David's illustrations before it went into production. A new and emerging writer, honors include Canadian Entrepreneur of the Year nomination and Chamber of Commerce nomination for Business Woman of the Year. Currently she is the National Coordinator of the Canadian Poetry Association.

The time was right, she was in the flow, and the rest will simply be.

David G. Repchuk

Born in the USA in 1954, he moved to Alberta Canada at the age of 12. David attended the Banff School of Fine Arts and spent 2 years in Europe and France creating art, and the last 20 years defining his style. He met Tracy in the computer industry, and moved to the Toronto area from Vancouver in 1992. His creations vary from pen and ink, pastel, acrylic, oil and watercolor. Currently a member of the Canadian Federation of Artists, Burlington Art Centre, Burlington Fine Arts Association, Hamilton & Region Arts Council, Flamborough Studio Artists, and is a board of director for Arts Milton and arts liaison for the Fine Arts Society of Milton.

Tracy is married to David Repchuk, they have 3 light sources; Kennedy Aviel (1995), Celestial Alyssa (1996) and Caleb Alexander (1997). The live in Kilbride, Ontario on a beautiful 16 acre paradise that inspires and infuses tranquility. Life philosophy of actualization is Dynamic Optimism Cultivating New Opportunistic Thought (DOCNOT).

New Style Focus

I love to discover new things, and recently found a poet that had created and expanded to formulate a new style of haiku poetry. With this creativity, we honor a future stylist of today.

Wayne Scott Ray

Shashin-Kaku Haiku – In Japanese;
Shashin – means photograph
Kaku – means picture (to sketch or draw)

Purpose:
To paint a picture that will leave a very strong impression on the mind of the reader. A photograph that says everything. Subjective, maudlin ideas and rhyme are not accepted. Must make a clear statement about life and the world around us.

Rules:
The **first line** is made up of 2 words of no more than 3 syllables or two feet. It must let the reader know what you want to talk about, and it must be connected to the second line in continuity of thought.
The **second line** is made up of up to 6 syllables or three feet and acts as an ending thought to the first line and must show no contrast.
The **third line** is the contrast line with less syllables than in the second line, two to three feet (5 syllables).

pay day
my kids eat from crushed tins
lucky dice fail me

For more details visit: www.mirror.org/wayne.ray/